FOUNDATIONS

A BIBLICAL VIEW FOR ALL OF LIFE

LEADER'S GUIDE

JOSEPH BOOT

WITH NATE WRIGHT & MICHAEL THIESSEN

Ezra

Interior and cover design by Jordan Cecile.

ISBN 979-8-9916932-6-4

Published by Ezra Press, an imprint of the Ezra Institute.
ezrainstitute.com

Printed in the United States of America.

CONTENT

INTRODUCTION

Christianity is not private therapy nor a weekend diversion. From the apostolic declaration that Jesus is Lord—a public claim with seismic implications in the Roman world—through the patristic defense of orthodox faith, the formation of medieval Christendom, and the magisterial reformation's recovery of Scripture's authority over church and commonwealth, Christians have confessed the Gospel as public truth. It announces the incarnate, crucified, risen, and ascended Christ who reigns over all. The Puritan vision of a godly commonwealth and the neo-Calvinist insistence of Kuyper and Bavinck that no sphere lies outside Christ's sovereignty further reveal the Gospel's cultural breadth. By contrast, reducing religion to the private and therapeutic is a modern, Enlightenment-era invention.

At the Ezra Institute, we labor to recover this reformational vision—the Gospel of the Kingdom—which summons men and women to comprehensive obedience to God's Word. *Foundations* serves this end by grounding believers in the whole counsel of God and equipping the church to think and live Christianly in every sphere of life.

This curriculum fits naturally into membership classes, discipleship cohorts, evangelistic studies, men's and women's groups, and student gatherings. Groups of eight to twelve participants cultivate the richest engagement: discussion, prayer, mutual accountability, and genuine fellowship. Seekers, new believers, and mature Christians alike can grow side by side under Scripture's guidance.

At its core, *Foundations* begins with a simple but far-reaching conviction: Christianity rests on God's own self-revelation. The truth of God—His creation and its order, humanity, sin, redemption, the church, and her mission—speaks with divine authority into every aspect of life. Doctrine naturally gives rise to worship and obedience; it shapes character, directs praise, and structures culture. As participants submit their minds and lives to Scripture, the Lord dismantles shallow, privatized religion and reorders worship and work, family and education, art and science, law and culture—bringing all things under the lordship of Christ.

May the Lord deepen your love for Christ, strengthen your confidence in His Word, and mobilize you for joyful obedience in discipling the nations—beginning with your own household and community—for His glory and your neighbor's good.

JOSEPH BOOT

PRESIDENT, EZRA INSTITUTE

LECTURERS

DR. JOSEPH BOOT

PRESIDENT, EZRA

PASTOR NATE WRIGHT

CANADIAN DIRECTOR, EZRA

DR. MICHAEL THIESSEN

US CHIEF OF OPERATIONS, EZRA

3 WAYS TO USE THE CURRICULUM

Foundations: A Biblical View for All of Life was designed with flexibility at its core, recognizing that every church, small group, and ministry has unique needs. You can engage with the material in its original three-week format, slow down for a more reflective six-week journey, or dive in through an immersive weekend intensive.

Built around three core teaching videos with guided processing and discussion questions, the curriculum gives you freedom to set the pace. Whether you're leading an adult Sunday School class, facilitating a small group, studying as a family, or hosting a church conference, *Foundations* adapts to your context and helps you think Christianly about every area of life.

OPTION 1: 6-WEEK COURSE (EXPANDED ENGAGEMENT)

Ideal for: Small groups, semester study, or church training class.

Format: One session per week, 60–75 minutes per session.

Strength: Allows more time for reflection, discussion, and gradual absorption.

Week 1 — The Cultural Crisis (Part 1)

- Walk through *Preparation, Prayer, and Probing Questions* together as a group (20 min).
- Watch the first half of *Video 1: The Cultural Crisis*. Pause at 13:06 (13 min).
- Reflect on the phrase "Jesus is Lord over all creation" by answering Discussion Questions 1–9 (30 min).
- Complete *Live It Out This Week* on your own at home.

Week 2 — The Cultural Crisis (Part 2)

- Walk through *Preparation, Prayer, and Probing Questions* together as a group (20 min).
- Watch the second half of *Video 1: The Cultural Crisis*. Start at 13:07 (16 min).
- Reflect on the difference between living with *vertical accountability* versus *horizontal relativity* by answering Discussion Questions 10–17 (30 min).
- Complete *Live It Out This Week* on your own at home.

Week 3 — The Religious Roots of Culture (Part 1)

- Walk through *Preparation, Prayer, and Probing Questions* together as a group (20 min).
- Watch the first half of *Video 2: The Religious Roots of Culture*. Pause at 13:23 (13 min).

- Reflect on the definition of culture as *"religion externalized"* by answering Discussion Questions 1–8 (30 min).
- Complete *Live It Out This Week* on your own at home.

Week 4 — The Religious Roots of Culture (Part 2)

- Walk through *Preparation, Prayer, and Probing Questions* together as a group (20 min).
- Watch the second half of *Video 2: The Religious Roots of Culture*. Start at 13:24 (16 min).
- Reflect on *structure and direction* by answering Discussion Questions 9–12 (15 min).
- Do the group exercise: Discussion Questions 13–14 (15 min).
- Complete *Live It Out This Week* on your own at home.

Week 5 — Transforming Culture for Christ (Part 1)

- Walk through *Preparation, Prayer, and Probing Questions* together as a group (20 min).
- Watch the first half of *Video 3: Transforming Culture for Christ*. Pause at 14:18 (14 min).
- Reflect on the calling to transform culture by answering Discussion Questions 1–4 (30 min).
- Complete *Live It Out This Week* on your own at home.

Week 6 — Transforming Culture for Christ (Part 2)

- Walk through *Preparation, Prayer, and Probing Questions* together as a group (20 min).
- Watch the second half of *Video 3: Transforming Culture for Christ*. Start at 14:19 (13 min).
- Reflect on *structure and direction* by answering Discussion Questions 5–11 (30 min).
- Complete *Live It Out This Week* on your own at home.

OPTION 2: 3-WEEK COURSE (INTENSIVE DIVE WITH FOCUSED SESSIONS)

Ideal for: Small groups, adult Sunday School, or discipleship cohorts.

Format: One session per week, 90–120 minutes per session.

Strength: Offers depth in a short time, great for a focused mini-series.

Week 1 — The Cultural Crisis

- Complete *Preparation, Prayer, and Probing Questions* on your own before the session.
- Watch *Video 1: The Cultural Crisis* (30 min).
- Engage in group discussion using Discussion Questions 1–17 (60 min).
- Complete *Live It Out This Week* individually at home.

Week 2 — The Religious Roots of Culture

- Complete *Preparation, Prayer, and Probing Questions* on your own before the session.
- Watch *Video 2: The Religious Roots of Culture* (30 min).
- Discuss together using Discussion Questions 1–7 (30 min).

- Do the group exercise: Discussion Questions 8–14 (20 min).
- Complete *Live It Out This Week* individually at home.

Week 3 — Transforming Culture for Christ

- Complete *Preparation, Prayer, and Probing Questions* on your own before the session.
- Watch *Video 3: Transforming Culture for Christ* (30 min).
- Engage in group discussion using Discussion Questions 1–11 (60 min).
- Complete *Live It Out This Week* individually at home.

OPTION 3: WEEKEND INTENSIVE

Ideal for: Conferences, retreats, or leadership training.

Format: Weekend (Friday night + Saturday), 90–120 minutes per session.

Strength: Great for intensive immersion, high engagement, and group bonding.

Sample Schedule:

Session 1 — The Cultural Crisis (90 min) – Friday Night

- Complete *Preparation, Prayer, and Probing Questions* on your own before the session.
- Watch *Video 1: The Cultural Crisis* (30 min).
- Engage in group discussion using Discussion Questions 1–17 (60 min).
- Complete *Live It Out This Week* individually at home.

Session 2 — The Religious Roots of Culture (90 min) – Saturday Morning

- Complete *Preparation, Prayer, and Probing Questions* on your own before the session.
- Watch *Video 2: The Religious Roots of Culture* (30 min).
- Discuss together using Discussion Questions 1–7 (30 min).
- Do the group exercise: Discussion Questions 8–14 (20 min).
- Complete *Live It Out This Week* individually at home.

Lunch Break

Session 3 — Transforming Culture for Christ (90 min) – Saturday Afternoon

- Complete *Preparation, Prayer, and Probing Questions* on your own before the session.
- Watch *Video 3: Transforming Culture for Christ* (30 min).
- Engage in group discussion using Discussion Questions 1–11 (60 min).
- Complete *Live It Out This Week* individually at home.

THE CULTURAL CRISIS

PREPARATION

Before watching the session, prepare your heart and mind with Scripture, prayer, and reflection.

READ & MEMORIZE

He is the image of the invisible God, the firstborn over all creation. For everything was created by Him, in heaven and on earth, the visible and the invisible, whether thrones or dominions or rulers or authorities—all things have been created through Him and for Him. He is before all things, and by Him all things hold together. He is also the head of the body, the church; He is the beginning, the firstborn from the dead, so that He might come to have first place in everything.

Colossians 1:15-18

OPTIONAL VERSE

All things were created through Him, and apart from Him not one thing was created that has been created. Life was in Him, and that life was the light of men. That light shines in the darkness, yet the darkness did not overcome it.

John 1:3-5

PRAYER FOCUS

1. Ask God to give you clarity about current cultural issues.

2. Pray that He would reveal any areas of compromise in your thinking or living.

3. Pray for courage to obey Christ in all areas of life.

4. Intercede for your church and leaders, asking that they would not conform to secular culture but to Christ.

PROBING QUESTIONS

1. What do I think the Gospel is mainly about?

_____

2. How would I currently define the word "culture"?

_____

3. When I think of the phrase "Christ is Lord," what areas of life come to mind?

_____

As you watch the video in session one, you can follow along and fill in the blanks.

1. THE OPENING

A. What does Scripture say about Christ as the Word?

"All things were made _____ [through] Him, and without Him, _____ [nothing] was made that was made." (John 1:3 NKJV)

B. Who is transforming whom today?

☐ The church is transforming culture

☑ Culture is transforming the church

☐ Neither

☐ Both

C. What does Paul say the Gospel concerns?

The Gospel concerns _____ [all] things.

D. What is at stake if we misunderstand this truth?

_____

_____

Hint: If we misunderstand that the Gospel concerns all things, we may start dividing life into "spiritual" and "secular" areas, limiting Christ's authority. This opens the door to compromise, allowing the culture to shape how we think, live, and lead—rather than the Word of God. In doing so, we risk disobedience and miss the power of the Gospel to transform every part of life.

2. THE NEED FOR STRUCTURE

A. In both city and countryside, how is God's order visible?

- Urban: Streets, _____ [commuting], people working, _____ [studying], and building.

- Rural: Farmers _____ [planting] and _____ [harvesting] with knowledge and precision.

B. What does this observable structure tell us about God?

☐ He prefers chaos

☐ He designed things to work without us

☑ He is a God of order and purpose

3. RECOGNIZING THE CRISIS

A. Three words describing our current moment:

"Moral, _____ [cultural], and _____ [ethical] upheaval."

B. How do many Christians feel today?

Many feel _____ [uneasy], _____ [confused], and unsure how to respond.

C. Why is it hard to name what's happening?

☐ We lack historical knowledge

☐ We're afraid of being offensive

☑ We often don't have a biblical framework for understanding culture

4. THE GOSPEL IS COSMIC IN SCOPE

A. According to Colossians 1, Christ created and holds together _____ [everything].

B. Paul says God reconciles not just some things, but _____ [all] things through Christ.

C. The Gospel reverses the curse of sin _____ [everywhere] it has touched.

D. We are commanded to preach the Gospel to all _____ [creation].

E. The "map" analogy teaches that if we don't see the big picture...

☐ We'll miss church

☑ We won't understand how to navigate the world

5. RELIGION, FIRST PRINCIPLES, AND SOCIETY

A. The word "religion" means to _____ [tie] or _____ [bind] together.

B. Biblically, religion is rooted in the _____ [heart], which is the center of man.

C. G.K. Chesterton said that abandoning first principles leads to _____ [madness].

D. Nietzsche's rejection of God led to _____ [insanity]—a picture of today's culture.

6. THE RISE OF RADICAL AUTONOMY

A. Radical autonomy = the belief that we belong to _____ [ourselves] and define truth on our _____ _____ [own terms].

B. What has been replaced as our cultural foundation?

☐ The Bible

☐ Reason

☑ God's vertical authority has been replaced with horizontal human contracts

C. List 3 examples of issues stemming from radical autonomy:

_____ [eg. Gender and Sexual Identity Confusion]

_____ [eg. Breakdown of the Family]

_____ [eg. Moral Relativism in Law and Education]

7. COMPROMISE IN THE CHURCH

A. Many churches today prioritize _____ _____ [cultural approval] over biblical faithfulness.

B. Popular slogans used to justify compromise include:

• "God is a God of _____ [love], not judgment."

• "Don't be a _____ [hater]."

• "Judge not, or you will be _____ [judged]."

8. GOD'S LAW & THE GOSPEL

A. Sin is defined as _____ [lawlessness]—breaking God's law.

B. Satan is referred to as the _____ _____ [lawless one] in 2 Thessalonians.

C. Paul says the law is for the _____ [lawless] and the rebellious (1 Tim 1).

D. The Gospel and the law are not enemies, but a _____ [seamless] garment.

E. Why is it dangerous to separate Gospel grace from Gospel obedience?

_____

_____

Hint: Grace without obedience leads to cheap grace—a Gospel that forgives but doesn't transform. Obedience without grace leads to legalism. True Gospel living holds both together: grace empowers obedience, and obedience is the fruit of grace. Separating them distorts the Gospel and weakens Christian witness.

9. DISCUSSION QUESTIONS

With your group, discuss the following questions.

1. Is the idea that Jesus is Lord over all creation and every aspect of life and human societies a new idea for you, or is this something you have fully embraced?

_____

_____

Hint: Let them answer this question before proceeding to the follow-up questions.

2. Do you believe that most people who confess to being a Christian embrace the idea that Jesus is Lord of everything?

_____

Hint: As Ray Comfort illustrates, many Christians think Jesus is just a safety parachute for them when the plane goes down. They don't see Him as the captain of the plane.

3. Why is it dangerous to shrink the Gospel to just personal salvation?

Hint: This limits the application of scripture to a few topics and reduces our view of scripture from being sufficient as the "rule for all of life" to be "the rule for a small part of life."

4. Fill in the blank: If the Gospel is just about me going to heaven, then I might ignore…

☐ How I live at work

☐ My views on politics or education

☐ My family life

☑ All of the above

5. Write a sentence describing the Gospel as more than just salvation:

Hint: Romans 12 tells us to be no longer conformed to the patterns of the world, but to offer our bodies as living sacrifices. Christ came as redeemer and King. He is to be followed, and we are to be transformed. This means Christians have a vision for the world that includes its transformation.

6. What are some signs you see in society that confirm it is in moral, cultural, and ethical upheaval? Where do you see "madness" in society?

Hint: The permission structure for violence in America. The open celebration of evil behavior. The division in the church.

7. What cultural principles have replaced God's Word in the public square?

_____

_____

Hint: Evolution instead of creation. Spiritist slogans instead of The Ten Commandments. Human feelings trump morality. Sexual promiscuity is promoted instead of upholding marriage.

8. If Jesus is Lord of all, creation, life, society, government, culture, etc., why are we not witnessing Christ's supremacy in all aspects of our society today?

_____

_____

Hint: We don't see Christ's supremacy in society because we've reduced the Gospel to personal salvation, embraced human ideas over God's Word, misunderstood justice, and neglected our calling to advance His Kingdom in every area of life due to distraction and compromise.

9. When you think of the phrase "Christ is Lord," what areas of life come to mind? What areas didn't come to mind until listening to the video?

_____

_____

Hint: Are your thoughts captive to Christ concerning your finances, private imagination, marriage roles, children's education, parenting decisions, and identity (how you think about yourself, speak to yourself, reflect on your behavior, etc.)?

10. Joe talked about vertical accountability versus horizontal relativity—try to put that concept in your own words.

_____

_____

Hint: Vertical accountability means that everyone is accountable to God; non-Christians are held to the same standards as Christians. Repentance occurs when the non-believer agrees with God that he or she is a sinner; thus, the law of God confronts all people of sin, and it's a good thing for all people. The believer preaches law to offer grace. If non-Christians are not condemned by God's standards, they have nothing from which to escape.

Hint: Horizontal relativity means majority rules. Or the loudest person defines right and wrong. It ignores what the Bible teaches about people being totally depraved. However, God's Word is SO MUCH HIGHER than the most intelligent person.

11. Where have you seen horizontal relativity override vertical accountability in society?

_____

_____

Hint: Abortion, medical assisted suicide, soft on crime, marriage/divorce, family, sexuality.

12. What is the danger of defining morality by consent alone?

_____

_____

Hint: Many people will willingly join sin. Many people consent to participate in what they know to be wrong.

13. Where are you personally being pressured to conform?

_____

_____

Hint: Family members can be tempting. Pressure at work can be a real problem. Sports culture often is a lure. A friend's bad character can corrupt the good in you.

14. Who in your life hands you ultimatums if you don't align with their convictions?

_____

_____

Hint: Husband? Wife? Child? Parents? Employer? Employees? Professors?

15. Who actually shapes the way you see issues, is it Christ's Word—or someone else's word?

_____

_____

Hint: Husband? Wife? Child? Parents? Employer? Employees? Professors?

16. How does Col 1:15-23 teach that the Gospel is more than personal salvation?

_____

_____

Hint: He is supreme, he saves, THAT he might become supreme in everything on earth.

17. Was there a new idea that came out of this session that you found very compelling, or alternatively, that you are struggling with?

_____

_____

Hint: Allow people to process as they need.

LIVE IT OUT THIS WEEK

- Identify one area of life that you've kept separate from Christ's Lordship:

_____

_____

Hint: Finances, Entertainment, Social Media, Work Life, Parenting, Marriage, Friendships, Politics, Use of Time, Education, Physical Health, Rest and Sabbath.

- Surrender it to Christ in prayer and action.

- Share what you're learning with a friend or family member.

- Memorize Colossians 1:15–18 this week.

- Ask your pastor how your church is engaging with culture biblically.

THE RELIGIOUS ROOTS OF CULTURE

PREPARATION

Before watching the session, prepare your heart and mind with Scripture, prayer, and reflection.

READ & MEMORIZE

Therefore, brothers, by the mercies of God, I urge you to present your bodies as a living sacrifice, holy and pleasing to God; this is your spiritual worship. Do not be conformed to this age, but be transformed by the renewing of your mind, so that you may discern what is the good, pleasing, and perfect will of God.

Romans 12:1-2

OPTIONAL VERSE

I am not praying that You take them out of the world but that You protect them from the evil one. They are not of the world, as I am not of the world. Sanctify them by the truth; Your word is truth. As You sent Me into the world, I also have sent them into the world.

John 17:15-18

PRAYER FOCUS

1. Ask God to reveal how certain cultures are shaping your thinking more than His Word.

2. Pray that you would live faithfully under Christ's lordship in all areas of life.

3. Intercede for Christian leaders to boldly shape political culture with the Gospel.

PROBING QUESTIONS

1. In what ways do I assume culture is neutral?

_____

_____

2. Where in my life has culture shaped me more than Christ's Word? Where does Satan have a foothold in my thinking and living?

_____

_____

As you watch the video in session two, you can follow along and fill in the blanks.

1. WELCOME & INTRODUCTION

A. What foundational truth is at the heart of this session? Culture is not neutral. It is the external expression of our deepest _____ [worship].

2. DEFINING CULTURE BIBLICALLY

A. Fill in the blanks:

- The word "culture" comes from the Latin word meaning the cutting edge of a _____ [plow].

- "Colonus" means to _____ [inhabit].

- "Cultus" means _____ [worship].

B. Culture is always shaped by a society's _____ [religion], whether explicitly or implicitly.

C. Diversity in culture reflects diversity in what people _____ [worship].

3. OBSERVING CULTURE AROUND THE WORLD

A. Culture is expressed in what areas of life? (Check all that apply)

☑ Law

☑ Education

☑ Diet

☑ Dress

☑ Art

☑ Architecture

B. In the West today, what kind of culture dominates?

☐ Christian

☐ Islamic

☐ Hindu

☑ Humanistic/Secular

4. CULTURE AS WORSHIP IN ACTION

A. Culture is not optional. All people are culture-makers, because we are made in the image of a God we _____ [worship].

B. Creation becomes culture when humans…

- Take grapes and make _____ [wine].

- Take trees and build _____ [buildings].

- Use words to form _____ [literature].

- Express sexual identity through _____ [intimacy].

C. Where have you seen the illusion of neutrality pushed in cultural conversations?

_____

_____

Hint: Culture is never neutral—it always reflects a religious direction. The illusion of neutrality is often seen in areas like education, science, politics, or media, where secular values are presented as "neutral" or "objective."

5. STRUCTURE & DIRECTION

A. Match the term with its meaning (draw a line to connect):

Term	Direction
Structure	The spiritual trajectory of an action or institution
Direction	God's design or order for something

Correct Answers	Direction
Structure	→ God's design or order for something
Direction	→ The spiritual trajectory of an action or institution

Examples:

Marriage

- **Structure:** A lifelong covenant between one man and one woman

- **Direction:**

    - *In rebellion:* selfishness, manipulation, divorce, polygamy, or same-sex unions

    - *In obedience:* mutual love and respect, sacrificial leadership by the husband, willing submission by the wife, raising children in the fear and admonition of the Lord

Music

- Both Bach and Lady Gaga use the same musical _____ [structure], but their songs go in radically different moral _____ [directions].

6. NO NEUTRAL GROUND

A. Paul teaches in Romans 1 that people "exchange the _____ [truth] of God for a _____ [lie]".

B. This leads to a _____ [worship] exchange, which leads to _____ _____ [cultural decay].

C. Which is true:

☐ Culture is neutral

☐ Culture can be good or bad depending on how it's used

☑ Culture is always going in a direction—toward or away from Christ

7. REDIRECTING CULTURE

A. We are not simply to react to culture. We are to _____ [shape] it for the glory of God.

B. Christians are called to "make culture" in obedience to God by building _____ [marriages], _____ [churches], and _____ [schools] that glorify Christ.

C. The fall affected every area of life, but the Gospel is God's means of _____ [restoring] and _____ [redirecting] culture toward Him.

8. SOCIETAL BREAKDOWN = A RELIGIOUS CRISIS

A. Every cultural collapse begins with a change of _____ [gods].

B. List two current examples where cultural decline reflects a spiritual problem:

- _____

- _____

Hint: Gender confusion and identity politics, abortion and euthanasia, breakdown of marriage and family, Corruption and injustice in government, widespread anxiety, depression, and loneliness, etc.

9. DISCUSSION QUESTIONS

With your group, discuss the following questions.

1. What does it mean that culture is "religion externalized"?

_____

_____

_____

_____

Hint: Religious beliefs come to life in the real world. Ideas shape behaviors. Religion shapes cultural practices.

2. What are some different cultures you have experienced, and how did they reflect their religious foundations and their belief systems?

_____

_____

Hint: Hindu, Islamic, Christian, Jewish, Buddhism, Secular, Communist, etc.

3. Give one example of a culture you've seen shaped by a religion other than Christianity:

_____

_____

Hint: Hindu, Islamic, Jewish, Buddhism, Secular, Communist, etc.

4. What are the ways that we have already been secularized?

_____

_____

_____

Hint: Treating Sunday like just another day for errands or sports; accepting "my truth/your truth" instead of objective truth; assuming science and faith are separate; prioritizing personal comfort over sacrifice.

5. In what areas of life (education, politics, work, entertainment, family life) do you see Christians adopting secular patterns of thought without realizing it?

_____

_____

_____

Hint:
- *Education: Sending kids to schools that teach a godless worldview but never talking about it at home.*
- *Politics: Voting mainly for economic benefit instead of biblical justice.*
- *Work: Defining success only by salary or promotions, not faithfulness.*
- *Entertainment: Consuming shows/music that celebrate sin without discernment.*
- *Family Life: Letting busyness, sports, or screens replace worship and discipleship.*

6. How does this secularization lead people to depend more on their own reason than the Lord's wisdom?

_____

_____

_____

Hint: It actually leads us to conceptualize the world from a humanist/rationalist framework rather than what scripture says. In its worst forms, it leads to apostasy and unbelief. Where people no longer trust God and His Word. In its mild forms, it leads to trite slogans and the use of self-help/psychology/leadership maxims instead of scripture.

7. What does Proverbs 3:5 say about this issue?

Hint: "Trust in the Lord with all your heart, and do not lean on your own understanding." This means we cannot let cultural wisdom or our own logic override God's revealed truth.

8. Do you see how impactful this really is? Do you see how it might actually lead people completely astray from God's intentions? What would be the scriptural metaphor for this divide?

Hint: The parable of the two roads (Matthew 7:13–14).

9. Joe argues that, essentially, there is no neutral direction for the structure and for those who participate in a structure. Why can there be no neutral direction?

Hint: There is no inbetween. We so want to be neutral, but we can't. We don't want the spotlight on us, but when we say nothing or do nothing, we are actually a part of the problem. He who is not for me is against me. The depraved mind is always twisted by sinful motives. People suppress the truth when they are against God.

10. Where have you seen the illusion of neutrality pushed in cultural conversations?

Hint: We're told to be open-minded, elevate academic freedom, and leave the Bible out of practical life.

11. Why isn't it enough to just avoid culture altogether?

Hint: Because we make culture as we live. A culture will be created. Avoiding broader culture simply means allowing that culture to take over the world.

12. If Christ is not shaping our culture, who is? What would you say are the main influences upon our Western culture today?

Hint: Satan, Hollywood sexualization, secularism, social-media, new age, atheism, etc.

13. Exercise: Think about a group or organization you're familiar with—this could be something like a t-ball league, a book club, a sports team, or even a fire hall crew.

Use the space below to reflect on the culture of that group. Culture is often described as "religion externalized"—the lived-out values, priorities, and beliefs of a community.

Consider and write down:

- What kind of language does the group use?

- How does it plan and schedule its meetings or events?

- How are members taught or trained?

- What kinds of outcomes or achievements are celebrated?

- What are the formal or informal rules everyone follows?

- How does the group manage itself and promote its activities?

Once you've written your observations, reflect on this:

- Do these cultural traits align with God's Word and the Ten Commandments?

- Are there aspects that honor God? Are there any that might offend Him?

Be ready to discuss your thoughts with the group.

_____

_____

_____

_____

_____

_____

_____

_____

_____

Hint: Every group has a culture—its "religion externalized." For example, a football league may schedule games on Sundays (showing what it values most), use language like "All in for the team" or "No pain, no gain," and celebrate trophies, travel, and total devotion to the team. It upholds virtues like hard work, competitiveness, and fair play. These rhythms, rules, and celebrations all reveal what is being worshiped—so the key question is whether they align with God's ways or subtly pull hearts away from Him.

14. How would your life look different if we truly believed that every cultural action is a form of worship?

_____

Hint: Imagine if our activities were shaped by God's intentions. A league might refuse to schedule games on Sundays, encouraging families to honor worship and rest. Parents would be guided to balance commitments wisely, and celebrations would highlight honesty, gratitude, and Christ-like character more than trophies or wins. In this way, even something as ordinary as sports could reflect that every cultural action is ultimately an act of worship.

LIVE IT OUT THIS WEEK

A. Identify one cultural habit for each structure in your life that needs to be redirected toward Christ. Make sure you address lawless habits:

Personal Habits: _____ [eg. Self-indulgence or Prayerlessness]

Family Habits: _____ [eg. Disconnection or Entertainment-driven]

Neighborhood Habits: _____ [eg. Isolation or Indifference]

Work Habits: _____ [eg. Careerism or Dishonesty]

Church Habits: _____ [eg. Consumerism or Passivity]

Media Habits: _____ [eg. Overconsumption or Impurity]

Political Habits: _____ [eg. Idolatry or Apathy]

Educational Habits: _____ [eg. Indoctrination or Pragmatism]

Medical Habits: _____ [eg. Autonomy or Technocracy]

- Pray for the Holy Spirit to guide you in becoming a faithful culture-maker in your community.

- Find one way this week to actively apply your faith in a cultural space (workplace, school, media, etc.).

- Ask someone you trust: "How do you see me being influenced by culture more than by Christ?"

JOURNAL PROMPT

A. How does Christ's Lordship change the way I...

Parent?   _____

Vote?   _____

Spend money?   _____

Use media?   _____

Hint:

- **Parent:** *Your role as a parent becomes one of stewardship, not control. You're called to raise your children in the discipline and instruction of the Lord (Eph. 6:4), aiming for their hearts—not just behavior.*
- **Vote:** *Voting is no longer just a civic duty but a Kingdom act. You're called to seek righteousness and justice, applying biblical principles to public life—not just personal benefit or party loyalty.*
- **Spend money:** *Money isn't yours—it's God's. You're a steward, not an owner. Christ's Lordship means spending and giving in ways that reflect His priorities: generosity, care for others, and eternal investments.*

- **Use media:** *Media consumption becomes a matter of discernment. You no longer engage passively—Christ's Lordship means you filter what you watch, read, and share through a biblical lens, seeking truth, beauty, and virtue.*

B. How can I shape my family's culture to reflect Christ's Lordship more clearly?

_____

_____

Hint: Family culture is shaped by repeated habits, values, and conversations. Think about what fills your home—your schedules, media, mealtime conversations, discipline, and celebrations. Are these pointing your family toward Christ? Consider adding regular family worship, praying together, curating media intentionally, setting rhythms of rest, and practicing hospitality. Christ's Lordship means that your home becomes a place of joyful discipleship, not just survival or routine.

TRANSFORMING CULTURE FOR CHRIST

PREPARATION

Before watching the session, prepare your heart and mind with Scripture, prayer, and reflection.

READ & MEMORIZE

So now, kings, be wise; receive instruction, you judges of the earth. Serve the Lord with reverential awe and rejoice with trembling. Pay homage to the Son or He will be angry, and you will perish in your rebellion, for His anger may ignite at any moment. All those who take refuge in Him are happy.

Psalm 2:10-12

OPTIONAL VERSE

So that at the name of Jesus every knee will bow—of those who are in heaven and on earth and under the earth—and every tongue should confess that Jesus Christ is Lord, to the glory of God the Father.

Philippians 2:10-11

PRAYER FOCUS

1. Pray that your faith would move beyond theory and into obedient action.

2. Ask God to use your daily work and life for Kingdom transformation.

3. Intercede for government leaders to turn from self-rule to Christ's lordship.

PROBING QUESTIONS

1. Have I treated the Gospel as only personal salvation? If so, how?

_____

_____

2. Where do I see my own vocation as part of shaping culture for Christ?

_____

_____

3. What do I think "faithful cultural engagement" actually looks like in my vocation?

_____

_____

Hint: Faithful cultural engagement means using your work to influence culture toward Christ—shaping norms, values, and practices in your field to reflect His Lordship.

As you watch the video in session three, you can follow along and fill in the blanks.

1. FROM WORSHIP TO CULTURE

A. Fill in the blanks:

- If culture is the public expression of _____ [worship], then the Gospel must lead to true _____ [culture].

- This true culture is described in scripture as the _____ [Kingdom] of God.

B. Which is true:

☑ The Gospel affects our culture as much as it affects our souls.

☑ Christians were made to shape the world, not escape from it.

2. RETREAT OR REFORM

A. Why has the church lost cultural influence?

- We've retreated into a bubble of private _____ [piety].

- We've limited Christ's jurisdiction to just the _____ [church].

- We've ignored areas like education, law, medicine, and _____ [government].

B. What happens when we retreat?

_____

_____

Hint: Consider what happens to truth, justice, and culture when God's people stay silent or avoid standing for what's right. What fills the space when Christians step back?

3. BIBLICAL MODELS OF ENGAGEMENT

A. Match the servant of God with their act of cultural engagement (draw a line to connect):

Term	Direction
Moses	Refused to stop praying; shaped pagan court [Daniel]
Nathan	Confronted Pharaoh as a false god [Moses]
Daniel	Preached Christ to political rulers [Paul]
John the Baptist	Rebuked David for adultery [Nathan]
Paul	Confronted Herod about marriage [John the Baptist]

B. What do all these examples teach us?

- God expects His people to _____ [confront] sin and proclaim His _____ [truth] in public life.

4. A KINGDOM THAT CONFRONTS

A. Fill in the blanks:

- Jesus reminded Pilate: "You would have no _____ [authority]...unless it had been given you from above." (John 19:11)

- God commands kings to "kiss the _____ [Son]" (Psalm 2).

B. What does this mean?

Hint: Both verses remind us that all earthly power and authority come from God, not from human strength or position. Even rulers must submit to Christ's rule and acknowledge His ultimate authority.

C. Which is true:

☐ Christ's Lordship depends on human approval.

☑ God holds rulers accountable to His standard.

☐ We can be neutral toward Christ in politics or culture.

5. TWO CULTURAL DIRECTIONS

A. According to Joe Boot, there are only two cultural options:

- Worship of the _____ [Creator]

- Worship of the _____ [creature]

B. Give a modern example of creature-worship in culture:

_____

Hint: Think about ways people today honor or depend on created things—like nature, celebrities, technology, or personal freedom—instead of the Creator who made them.

C. How does Chesterton describe this danger?

"Abolish God and the _____ [government] becomes god."

DISCUSSION QUESTIONS

1. What stood out to you most of all in this last session?

_____

_____

Hint: a good spot to find out what they're thinking.

2. Joe repeated an important point at the start of the session, and it is worth repeating.

1. Culture is the public expression of the worship of a people.

2. The Gospel restores man to true worship.

3. Therefore the Gospel restores man to true culture.

What does the word "true" mean here? In other words, "true culture" is what kind of culture?

Hint: "True culture" reflects God's original design—it promotes righteousness, limits sin, cultivates goodness, and reveals beauty, order, and truth rooted in creation.

3. As stated during the video, Jesus reminded Pilate:

"You would have no _____ [authority]...unless it had been given you from above." (John 19:11) And God commands kings to "kiss the _____ [Son]" (Psalm 2). Now add, "All _____ [authority] has been given to me in heaven and on earth. Go, therefore, and make disciples of all nations, baptizing them in the name of the Father and of the Son and of the Holy Spirit, teaching them to observe everything I have commanded you. And remember, _____ [I am with you] always, to the end of the age." (Matthew 28:18-20)

What does this mean? How should it affect every conversation and every decision of our lives?

Hint: If I am in Christ and confident that I am representing the Bible carefully, I have authority over anyone who offers competing ideas that are hollow and deceptive. As Christ's ambassador, I have the authority to teach in the same way that He did.

4. What did Joe mean when he said we have ecclesiasticized the Bible?

Hint: This means limiting the authority of the scripture, and the Lordship of Christ to the institutional church and salvation, not holding the entire world accountable to Christ.

5. Joe also reminds us that when we limit the authority of scripture, the result is the marginalization of the Christian Church and its influence upon our culture. Can you think of historical examples of past Christian culture that stand in contrast to today's retreat?

Hint: The Christian abolition of slavery, the Puritan colonizing of America, and the Magna Carta.

6. What are some cultural structures that you are involved with (marriage, family, business, sports, music, art, science, education, government, etc.), and how are you influencing their direction?

Hint: Marriage, family, business, sports, music, art, science, education, government, etc.

7. Where do you see idolatry occurring within these structures today?

_____

_____

_____

_____

Hint: Idolatry shows up in many everyday structures. For example, local governments may idolize money, control, or political influence; families can worship comfort, entertainment, or leisure; children and students may place teachers or professors on a pedestal as the ultimate authority; workplaces often elevate success, productivity, or status above all else. These patterns reveal where trust and devotion are given to something other than God.

8. What fears do you have when you think about bringing God's Word to bear in your sphere of influence? What do you assume is at stake? And who are your primary opponents? In other words, who do you struggle to fear instead of fearing the Lord?

_____

_____

_____

_____

Hint: Fears may include losing your job, being mocked or excluded at work, upsetting family or fellow Christians, failing in evangelism, or being disliked or hated for your faith.

9. What steps can you take to bring God's Word to bear in your sphere of influence?

_____

_____

_____

_____

Hint: Change a policy, run for office, write an essay that honors Christ, share a bold Christian post online, or speak directly from God's Word instead of staying vague.

10. Which private area of your life do you most struggle to bring under Christ's rule?

_____

Hint: It could be online habits, music choices, political views, favorite activities, group affiliations, or even controlling your speech.

11. It was argued that all Christians are called to confront sin, expose idolatry and proclaim truth, but we are to do it with Truth and Grace. How do we ensure that we are not compromising either Truth or Grace?

_____

Hint: Both are defined in scripture.

Truth = honesty, Grace = kindness.

Our culture tries to force feed us to be too gracious to the point that we become deceptive. Our anger tendencies compel us to be impatient and lack understanding.

Question 1 to ask yourself – Am I lying right now? (because of cowardice, or because I fear confrontation)
Question 2 to ask yourself – Am I controlling my tongue, or am I out of control? (because I am being malicious to win the debate, or because I am angry without just cause)

Be aware of these points as you discuss this, because it's likely to be pulled away from truth and grace even as you begin to discuss it. Scripture is our guide in these areas, not human strategies for persuasiveness.

LIVE IT OUT THIS WEEK

- Identify one idol in your personal or local culture that needs to be challenged:

Hint: Think about areas where people place ultimate trust or devotion—like comfort, approval, success, entertainment, wealth, family, politics, or personal freedom—instead of God.

- Take one small step this week to confront it with grace and truth.

- Reflect on what faithful cultural obedience looks like in your job, home, or civic life.

- Pray Psalm 2 over your local leaders.

JOURNAL PROMPT

What would change in my daily habits if I truly believed Christ is King over my city, school, workplace, and nation?

Hint: If you truly believed Christ is King over every sphere, your habits would reflect that authority—more prayerful decisions, bolder witness, greater integrity, and intentional efforts to align your work, speech, and relationships with His rule. You'd live as an ambassador of His Kingdom in every setting.

Where have I been tempted to stay silent rather than speak God's truth into public life?

Hint: Think about moments when fear, comfort, or social pressure kept you quiet—conversations at work, school, online, or with friends—where speaking God's truth felt risky, awkward, or costly.

PREPARING FOR WHAT'S NEXT

This was the final session in the *Foundations* series. But Kingdom work continues.

Final Questions to Consider:

- Where has God placed me to make an impact?

- What issue has He burdened me to speak into?

- Am I more afraid of man's rejection or God's command?

Optional Reading

- Jeremiah 29:4–9

- Matthew 28:18–20

- Romans 13:1–7

Visit: www.ezrainstitute.com for more tools, resources, and training opportunities.